# Strange Animals

**Praise for *Strange Animals***

'*Strange Animals* takes you to wild places; from Lake Huron to Swansea bedsits. These are hungry poems; where she plays with all our senses, feeds us chips, Swiss roll, orange peel, Sunday roasts. Discover what she has learned about planting a garden, "the land will remember who it was before the garden". These poems will leave you full of hunger and love, a travel guide and love story; go with her, and let the "Aurora Borealis call you home".'
**– Jessica Mookherjee**

'Reading *Strange Animals* feels a bit like rummaging around in someone's well-travelled backpack full of old photographs, seashells, tarot, and countless precious found objects collected for "the passing of knowledge". A brilliant new voice.'
**– Roberto Pastore**

'Emily Vanderploeg's clear-eyed lyric poetry explores the questions of where we belong, who we have become, and who or what undertakes that journey alongside us. She reflects on a personal and familial history of immigration, acknowledging both the gift and the weight of that history. To read this intimate collection feels like being in conversation with a friend, allowing us the freedom to see ourselves anew, and to welcome our own continuous and surprising changes.'
**– Carolyn Smart**

'*Strange Animals* is a collection that moves deftly between different kinds of poetic looking: the close up of the personal and intimate, and the longing gaze towards far-away family, language, culture. These are poems of abundance even as they mourn what is lost, charting the reader through gardens and orchards, down urgent green rivers and through teeming swamps, and so often we see the sea – a means to anchor even as it separates the self from what matters most: "that far field". For all our wandering in the rich landscapes of a remembered natural world, we go inside, too, where another kind of richness awaits. These sharp and surprising poems so often put one in mind of Gwen John's interiors: the beauty and importance of the domestic, and the hard-won rewards found in the self alone. There is heartache here but also a committed hopefulness: these poems have faith that love can emerge in "the space between / the end and the beginning".'
**– Katherine Stansfield**

**Emily Vanderploeg** writes poetry, fiction, and reviews. She studied English and Art History at Queen's University (BA Hons) and Creative Writing at Swansea University (MA, PhD), and teaches creative writing to children and adults. Vanderploeg is a Hay Festival Writer at Work and recently completed a novel with the help of a Literature Wales New Writer's Bursary Award. Her poetry pamphlet, *Loose Jewels,* won the Cinnamon Press Pamphlet Competition and was published in 2020. Originally from Aurora, Ontario, Canada, she lives in Swansea with her two cats, Zsuzsi and Annie.

# Strange Animals

# Emily Vanderploeg

PARTHIAN

Parthian, Cardigan SA43 1ED
www.parthianbooks.com
First published in 2022
© Emily Vanderploeg 2022
ISBN 978-1-913640-70-5
Editor: Susie Wildsmith
Cover image by Lieke van der Vorst
Cover design by Emily Courdelle
Typeset by Elaine Sharples
Printed and bound by 4edge Limited, UK
Published with the financial support of the Welsh Books Council
British Library Cataloguing in Publication Data
A cataloguing record for this book is available from the British Library.

*For Mum and Dad*

# CONTENTS

## Orienteering

## Cupid and Psyche

## Strange Animals

## River Reading

*Notes*
*Acknowledgements*

# ORIENTEERING

# Orienteering

Let's make a map of summer in southern Ontario:
a route of spruce swamps and blueberry stands,
chip trucks down farm tracks marked
as signposts for tired railway towns
and sea-lake lookouts.

I'll trace creeks with the lines on my palm;
tell fortunes of life amongst the bulrushes.
The skeeters speak slow here; they're so quiet,
whispering about what the land remembers.
We'll leave the shouting to the black flies
and the ghosts of a northern town.

Three wild turkeys run towards nowhere –
can you draw the sweetness of twitch-grass and cedar?
If you trace that wind, I'll show you
when the thunderstorms are coming,
and when they do we'll follow the lightning
home.

# Itthon

The gambolling gait of Soviet trains
swaying past the soft kiss
of fine cakes on the tongue
tasted in a *cukrászda* where
men and women sip thick coffee
with a sigh at the propaganda paper
and the pastry cases
*dobos torta, Eszterházy, geszténye puré*
passing the time of day
when the watercolour sky ripples
in the glass of the Duna
and it is warm even
on nights when it is not.

Tell me, how do you feel here?

# On Christmas Eve

The trees are creaking,
rolling shoulders and cracking wrists.

The snow is not white, but clean
electric, a resting cheek.

Cloaked in grandmother's furs,
take the *pogácsa* from the oven, now hold
the hundred-year-old fork, soft silvered and bone handled,
lift herring from the *smörgåsbord*, suck sweet onions,
and guzzle back *Gewürztraminer* from tiny goblets.

I am smiling; the Aurora Borealis has called me home.
Over the stretching fields of Bethesda it is night,
the *kachelofen* is burning.

# Last night I dreamt of oranges

My thumb running over
smooth dimpled skin, like
pores on my face
when I observe myself
too closely
in mirrors.

In Florida we saw an orange
tree; heavy limbs hanging low
in the yard. Lips numbed by
endless orange Popsicles,
I am amazed:
fruit grows in February.

Madrid in March: mornings we eat
palmyras, potato tortilla, juice of *naranja*;
fresh-squeezed fruits from Seville.
This is how I taste Spain,
so sweet and thick with pulp.

Mum is pouring orange flower water
into buttercream. I declare boredom;
she hands me an orange.
Picking off white pith, I place the rind
in my mouth, an orange smile replacing
baby teeth.

# Things I Have Learned About Planting a Garden

Make a border of marigolds, alternating yellow and orange,
around the herbs and petunias to encourage the sun
and sweetness of your tarragon.

Plant yellow roses for friendship
one by the woodshed, another by the stoop.
Blushing pink at mid-summer, petals curl
arched backs in the heat, ready for love.

In the arid patch by the cornfield
cultivate two rows of wax beans
with tomatoes in between.
Ready to pick before Indian summer
when the cicadas are born and singing,
the *zöldbableves* will taste best
from brown, earthenware bowls.

Leave the raspberry bush alone
in the pampas beyond the beds
so berries may sweeten themselves
in a slow secret with the sugar maple,
and be happened upon by wise birds.

Let the saddest flowers grow freely –
forget-me-nots, phlox, lily-of-the-valley –
so that curious children will pick them for their mothers
and the land will remember who it was
before the garden.

# Can you hear her whistling in the orchard?

In my sleep I found an orchard:
blue plums, yellow pears,
an apple tree and prickling blackberries,
where I laid deep in long grass
the kind you can pick and pray with
or make kazoos, whistling at cicadas.

I unlocked the gate, running
for the farthest meadow,
where trees hummed silver
and the breeze whistled low,
low, low down into the field, *shh*,
*shh*, *shh*, she whispered.

On waking I cut the fruit to bake in a pie:
halved and quartered, hard but sweet;
brambles picked clean, I could taste the meadow's
cool sweet hum, when the gate was open
and I could reach it, that far field where
the silvered leaves shivered not from cold,
but from the strength of my approach.

# Whippoorwill

I am thinking about my childhood.

Or, maybe I am thinking of snow:

cold velour against my cheek
as I sprawl, breathless
in the gully of the gorge
having been thrown from a toboggan,
my boots still caught in its candy cane tongue;
beyond me the creek is frozen
but the pickerel are moving
beneath the ice, caught
and released last summer.

I am thinking about summer in my childhood.

At camp, my best sport is Arts and Crafts:
watch me weave bracelets of leather,
wield and scissor scraps of old dresses,
costumes from plays past, a patchwork
quilts the story of whippoorwills
and sandpipers, pioneers and lyrics
to songs never written down.

I am thinking of who I expected to become in childhood.

Or, how I have come to be:
living by trees and seas I cannot name
when my children ask and I blame
the gnathic undulations of seasons
that propel me forward, yet leave me
bewildered by the amount of time
that has passed –

Can I really be as old as I am?

Time is serpentine, twisting and tricking
me into new shapes that have nothing to do
with the texture of snow or the wax of crayons
melted in coffee cans to make the tools of survival.

I am thinking about growing up.

Or, maybe I am waiting for someone
to tell me I already have.

# Everywhere There is Snow

Except for where I am.
The polar vortex blows
over the streets and fields of my growing up
in Thinsulate mittens, snowpants swishing
with heart-shaped patches on the knees
sewn by my mother
who emailed me last evening:
*Deep freeze here!* and a photo –
the kitchen thermometer
-23°C, an icicle, a cardinal
red as lifeblood
in the snow.

*What kind of snow is it?*
I asked my friend in Bristol, as she assessed
whether her car could scale her driveway.
Is it soft or heavy, have the rabbit tracks
turned to slush, or can you dust the powder
from your hair?
Or is it packing snow, favoured by children
for snowballs and snowmen?
*Tell me what it sounds like.*
*Place the phone by your boot,*
I say, a catch in my throat –

the ache of an icy wind in my cheeks,
lungs opened by a frigid breath,
streaming eyes and nose; the sound
of tires swift on a frosted highway –
I tell my friend on the phone:
*Don't break, just slide into it,*
thinking of a night
17 years ago, just 17-years-old when
a car made a perfect figure 8

as if floating in slow motion
on a snow-blanketed suburban street
silent and empty and curiously warm.
The car halted neatly at a 4-way stop.
*Why did you do that?* I asked the boy driving.
Snow dusted down like icing sugar on the windshield.
*I didn't,* he said, and drove me home.

# The Sea is a Foreign Country

selecting a sky-blue pencil crayon
to colour in 8"x11" Mercator maps, seven seas
sold to us as oceans, always oceans

vast and frightening and far away
the Atlantic, we were told, is our ocean
by proximity; a tenuous connection

the St. Lawrence Seaway gives way
to freshwater folk like us
salt and French on the tongue when

we travel to watch whales
because they are threatened, joy feels like
pain when they crest the surface

in fascination of seashells, collecting zebra mussels
at Lake Simcoe, I swore they hid pearls
before slicing heels and choking waterways

in Florida I first felt skin salted
tight and itchy; I stole true seashells in a bucket
retreating back to swimming pool chlorine

more comfortable than aggressive waves, Australian
riptides gripping my ankles like the undertow
that nearly drowned my mother in Pacific Acapulco

yet I could nap peacefully in the sun
on Lake Balaton, a familiar cradle, as if it were
Lake Huron's opposite shore

so Swansea is an ocean place, despite being called
the sea, lakes have margins, bodies of water drawn
by bodies made of water on children's maps

# In Praise of Great Lake Swimmers

You've set your mind to it,
the distance and the pace boat,
sips of orange juice; slick cold skin.
Front crawl or breaststroke
a lithograph or tin plate; folk songs
for remembering that Huron has the bluest water.

Beware the menace of Superior, if you believe the ballads.
So frigid and hostile, she makes her own wind –
a woman's lake that swallows ships and men.
Should have tried Huron first, come to think of it:
party at Wasaga Beach, or a good old-fashioned
protest at Bruce Nuclear Station.
Yeah, why don't you make it about something?
Mention the escarpment; the eroding bluffs.
Throw in a Niagara stunt, raise money, risk
arrest. Swim from Manitoba to Quebec.

No, skip Michigan. That's not our lake.
Make a point of Erie (folks always forget Erie).
Schedule your rest break
with the lampreys and pickerel.
Have you seen inside a lamprey's mouth?
Teeth a Chinese finger trap
waiting to latch onto and suck the blood
of nudists at Hanlan's Point.

Ah, yes, Ontario, you're almost there!
All the way to Buffalo – did the Americans greet you
with a banner and 21-gun salute?
Well then, come home, Swimmer.
Gamble a spell in Gananoque, follow the whales
up the cold St. Lawrence, gasping,
drift across the salted Atlantic to finally

wash up on a Gower beach
and say:

*I am too tired to swim back.*
*This will be my home now.*
*Take care of the lakes*
*and my mother and father*
*for me.*

# Bears Only Want to Love Their Children

I am Hungarian
        – mark my cheekbones
I am Dutch
        – check my sweet tooth
I am Swedish
        – blonde-haired in a cold snap
I am German
        – by my mother's maiden name
And great-granny was Transylvanian
        – if you trust the make of your map

*

*What about the gypsies?*

Stealing children isn't worth the price of meat.

*What about the rising seas?*

Our people prefer to be landlocked.

*What about the painted horses?*

We only take them out at Christmas.

*What about the rituals?*

Someone, somewhere back a Slovak, a Romanian, too
but oh no, not us, not ever, a Jew.

*What about the vampires?*

They're more interested in embroidery and wheat.

*

*But what about the bears?*

Ontario 1962.
My father's cousin wrestled one.
Does that make the Canadian more true?

They taught us Bear Safety at camp:
leave your sugar and shampoo by the lake,
hoist your supper up a tree,
sing songs along the bush trails
and the bears will leave you be.

# Meeting Emily Carr in the Bush

I follow her through underbrush,
telling not asking questions:

How do you make paint move
even after it dries.
Why do I flee every time,
never waiting
for the river to flow again.

She is not interested in speaking to me.
Examines her brush, the trees, the totem.

In her silence is a path:

when I am done with words
                                    I may swim home
to paint with
            earth and berries
                                                crushed
                        between ink-stained fingers but
until then
                        my canvas must remain
                            stitched to my back.

# National Parks and Reserves

Let's honeymoon deep
in the woods of Yellowstone,
draw our marriage bed
in cartoon outlines.
We'll set our watches by Old Faithful
and paint our life in Technicolor™,
Yogi Bear and Cindy Bear and a feast
of pic-a-nic baskets, the table laid
with the Russian silver Grandpa gave me
when he came by for tea on Sunday.

Can you hear that?
The passing of knowledge;
that's the sound of a flood in Yosemite:
Bridal Veil, Horse's Tail,
what romantic named the falls?
Bugs Bunny, outwitting us all,
deep in valleys with long views
of wizened sequoias and hot springs.
*That's Wagner, before that, Liszt,*
I know this, thinking only of Grandpa
grinning sagely at the Looney Tunes.
This is how our love story will be told
when we are gone and the value
of photographs is examined by youths
only for the paper they're printed on.

And the loon at Algonquin
swims by with its baby on its back –
*Did you know that loons are beacons*
*for the cleanliness of water?* –
No thanks to Cyril Sneer,
even as we listen to The Racoons' call
to *run with us*, these children

we summon, name, and bear,
who will collect our possessions gladly
when we pare down, preparing to die.
*Would you like a cut-glass candy dish?*
The black chicks balance, growing their lives
with our curios and then they can say,
*this belonged to my grandfather*
and visitors will nod with appreciation,
at the life bought, drawn, and collected
in the old growth forests of North America.

# My uncles are dying

There is mist over sunflower fields,
a cool day in September
on the Communist train to Szolnok.

The compartment, all rusted glass, a Polaroid frame:
Rákoskert, snap.
Sülysáp, snap.
Újszász *nem a végállomást.*

Rows of bent heads
brown and stiff, stalks slick now –
the mist will be rain by evening.

Why didn't anyone cut them, harvest and salt the seeds?

Before the track weed turned to yarrow, before
the pain in the stomach was called cancer,
a left arm clutched, shoulders slackened
(he only spoke a minute before).

Faded paper castles curl above the window
that will not latch.
*Következő megálló –*

we are late for the festival.

# tan-renga and a haiku, for Nigel

a summer of rain –
not a door in this house
will shut without a shove

*green wood*
*too early for a fire*

\*

long enough in one town
to notice the people's
ways of aging

*too slow*
*too soon*

\*

just when I think
this is how alone I am
– a shadow, watching

# Waiting for the Funeral

Twice I've found your daughter,
at the Tav, and again, in town.

We wore duffel coats,
spoke too long in doorways,
laughed at the absurdity of body bags,
wanted you.

What comes next?
It is still too early for daffodils.

# Loose Jewels

Mum, remember your moss gardens
gathered from the bush by the railroad tracks?
You'd take the dog with you, Puli or Vizsla
bred for that other life we might have known,
seen on Super 8: wild boar in the hills
of Miskolc, smoke from the hunters' fire,
*zsíros kenyér* and carved bone pipes.

But Grandpa took after his mother
who owned the movie theatre, before
the Russians came, put her money into loose jewels,
later sewn into his pockets before he fled in the night,
so that you could make shrines upon the supper table:
your mother would water them and they'd stay alive for weeks.

Grandpa paid somebody to tend his mother's grave,
while we, the ancestors, stayed busy an ocean away.
Who washed the stone, lit a candle in a red glass jar
and prayed on All Saint's Day?

Today your mother is ash, feeding the moss
of three gardens in York Region
as I stroll Nefelejcs utca, peering in at the flower sellers.
I would choose chrysanthemums (she always said
they were funeral flowers). *Kezit csókolom kívánok*
the gatekeeper greets me, mistaken for a local
mourner. *Temető* tourist, we never lost anybody
in the wars, only minds and fortunes
but those can be rebuilt.

The last Thanksgiving before she forgot
how to bring a fork to her lips,
Grandma smiled at me, held my hand,
looked at our matching crooked fingers and said,

'We were so worried that the Russians would rape us';
she who stood on her head daily, studied psychology
at sixty, stretched strudel dough by hand,
preventing tears by twisting round her rings
made from those loose jewels
glinting on my twin fingers,
as I read inscriptions on cracked stones.

*Édesanya*, when did the payments stop?

The grey-green lichens grow thick and brittle here,
and it is 1983 and I am born
and it is 1963 and you are making moss gardens
and it is 1943 and my grandmother is hiding
in a basement, afraid, for three months
and she doesn't know that she will have
a daughter who gives her living things,
or that even as ash, she will still be
tending our gardens.

# CUPID AND PSYCHE

# Fall in Love

No, not the easy heat of summer –
that's for lust, tanned skin dalliances,
fluorescent nights and sly half-smiles.

Spring's balmy wet is for birth,
the heady copulation of animals,
and the death of the once-beloved.

Winter is for sleep and endurance,
the false push of February needed
to remind lovers who lies next to them,
until light returns to mornings
and they blink, mole-eyed into the sun.

But look, there are roses in our cheeks,
smell the undersong of leaves.
Fevered kisses in fallow fields:
this is when we will conceive our children.

The crunch of an apple, shared between two –
come closer, hook your arm in mine,
nights are getting colder,
find the heavy blankets.

# Old Brown Coat

Soft corduroy covers
the limp body of a stricken doe
waiting to be carried from the side of the road.

*You don't have to say I told you so*
she howls at the touch of a hand on her back
this cold September night of dim light
empty pints and picnic tables
rotted by old rains.

Fevered wet eyes frantic and afraid
search for the lost warmth
of a love. Unbearable
exposure to the elements
of being left behind.

*I would never say that*
the giver of the hand says
wrapping the body tightly
in silver buttons and a sad laugh.
At last the creature weeps and sleeps soundly
for the first of a winter of nights.

# Parade

I heard you got everything you wanted.
It all fell perfectly into place.

They wiped your debts and you found your Goa.
The football pitches of the East were suitably picturesque.
You stopped using people, took up drugs again,
got your eyes fixed and got married –

I saw your wedding picture on
mylifeisbetterthanyours:
it was sunset, you were older,
we didn't know each other at all.

# Paper Cut

I never wrote you a love poem.
I wrote us a novel instead.
With you as the

better man
(that you always said you wanted to be)
and me with my happy ending.

Your sister still turned to Jesus
even in the final draft

and your arrogance and my anxiety
were nobody's fault
just plot devices.

Oh, how I loved you –
you liar, you stranger,
you rented soul.

# Solstice

With forehead pressed to cool glass
I think of you –
Welsh rains and the ache of damp houses,
the soft heat of your bed
and the absence of fear
in your presence.

You are my solstice:
the return of light
in my vision, still cloaked
with that other year's end.

\*\*\*

the thought of you
savoured like hard
candy in the mouth –
slippery sugar tongue
fooling around, smooth
shell clicking against eye teeth
wanting
to crack the surface, uncover
that soft jewel-coloured centre
but – swallowing the juice of sweet patience
for seven-and-a-half weeks
of summer heat, your face
at the crest of a mountain, my feet
on two sides of a sea and
**the thought of you**

# Is there such a thing as a sun storm?

It was bright and hot, but I'm sure that there was thunder,
my heart still warm from yours, warming.

My daydreams decode your looks and lyrics,
though each time we meet is a refrain:

you are strumming
I am tapping trees

And I've been singing the same three songs
since the last full moon
when we stood on your doorstep,
spying through the trees, whispering,
as if we'd disturb her.

*Please, will you decide to love me?*

This waiting sky is pink at the edges;
sap is running sweet:

come home now
buds are bursting – let's build a house
come home.

# Cupid and Psyche

spy on each other yet
there is too much seeing
at stake, so they stalk
social media, a 'like' here,
a day and night of deep scrolling
there, looking for signs of new lovers
and likely encounters
with mutual friends.

Psyche feigns indifference.
Cupid leaves Psyche on 'seen'.
She is wary and watchful, still loves
the drama of it all
when he lurks in the views
of 24-hour stories, and a messenger offers
a green-lit glimpse of him.

He waits for her
to reach for him in the night
with blue light and chiming bells,
those old, sweet feelings, inviting him
to don wings, take flight, and shoot
one last arrow
to drain her
swollen heart.

# In the Land of Fairies

a hundred years passed in an instant
sleeping deep inside
the comfort of sadness

at least there were no gifts
or offers of food. I remained hungry

until, a dream of milk:

even though she was sour ,
cap-crusted and out of date;
a note attached: do not throw away

while I, just enough left to cut
tea's bitterness, nearly used up by him
biding his time in sadness, too

until finally, I woke, found
an ironstone in a river, a fossilized star,
to barter my way out of being
his second choice.

# What season do the buzzards come?

The cactus keeps growing
by winter light and man-made heat.
It taunts with fuchsia flowers;
rarely asks for drinks.
I rub my flaking skin,
brush the salt from my boots.

See the white strands coming in
quick and sleek at my temples?
The TV's on for company
and the fat spits from the pan.

*Count your blessings*
*ungrateful girl, wilful nomad –*
*you, with your deserts in cold climates,*
*be patient, be sacred,*
*sharpen your teeth on a porcupine*
*and weigh the salt of your years.*

Tea burns my tongue
and I'm singing my poets,
*oh Joni, oh Stevie, oh oh oh –*

The terracotta pots have cracked
from too little heat, too little affection.

# Are you hungry?

Yes. No. I don't know.

*If you could have anything right now*
*what would it be?*

A hand to hold.

*What do you want for supper?*

Someone to ask me,
'Shall we go out? Or
cook something nice together?'

*What would you like for dessert?*

Another heat in my bed.

*Have you been fed?*

No. Yes. I don't know.

*Are you hungry?*

Always.

# On meeting in the lane, a year after we last spoke

I look up at the windows of houses
instead of out to sea.

Take pans from the oven with a thin tea towel,
burning my fingertips.

Eat Swiss roll for supper
licking the artificial cream like
it is your tongue in my mouth.

Accept the glass of red wine
*which you know gives me lust and headaches*
when I have dinner with you
*which I shouldn't have agreed to.*

# Rivulets

Meeting at the point of moons,
I'd read your fortune,
                    find the heart line
faint across your palm.

That first November,
the nightly downpour
                    felt like love
even as rivulets ran down backtrack stairs,
        I thought,
there will always be        another summer.

All that

                    time

I didn't know
            it was me
                    who was meant to build
                            the house.

# After Quarantine

I said, we'll go crabbing,
on the sandy flats of the estuary,
bootlegging moonshine and starshine
in eggplant purple dark.
The sun will be in Cancer,
when it is full of hope,
never even considering summer
could end.

Patiently, I watched our correspondence
meander day to day,
plinking-popping messages:

What have you baked?
*Any progress on the paperback*
*you're writing?*
Did you know that this #
is called an 'octothorpe'?
*I love oranges.*
Do you really like to sing?
*I am thinking of joining*
*a peristeronic society*, you told me,
*pigeons are very misunderstood birds.*

Yes, I replied. They mate for life.

*Do they? Terrifying.*

Remember when we saw them
picking chips with salt and vinegar
from the bin outside my window?

They were starving; heart muscle weak
but rushing in, ready for roosting.

*I guess having children is something I'd try…*

For so long I believed
there was sweetness
in the lethargy of your love.

# Leftovers

I'll keep Sunday's roast for tomorrow's supper
and the passing thoughts of us
drunk in a playhouse kitchen;
the vigorous way he used to stir the gravy
arms tense and hard like when he held me
on cold nights and closer
in the heat of his leaving.

I'll keep an image of myself wearing red
in a warm cavern bar; I put my hand in his pocket
reapplied red lipstick, reminded everyone
that I am the Queen of Wands when I want to be
and will be when there are spare hours again.

I'll keep being called beautiful by a man
I'd never noticed noticing me.
*What do you remember about me?* I asked, unkindly.
*Your face,* he said, *I remember your beautiful face* –
almost a question, as if I'd been hiding myself
all along.

I'll keep the vision of the capsized plain
from the window of the train to Kecskemét
and myself a mother to a daughter named Katalin
while a herd of deer, white-tailed and stampeding
across higher ground, leave the field lake
and my womb to the laughing geese.

# You Never Asked

So, I never say it.

That I would be a good mother.

That I have always seen myself
as the best mother
to my little girl, and boy, and girl
who exist
only in a future's dream.

It has never been
indecision. I haven't waited, or put it off.

It's not what you think.

I have only wanted
love    an equal partner    a mistake, even
but want is not the means to conception.

Perhaps, I will always be
alone.

Perhaps, somehow, I wanted this,
too.

# Ruby

When did the night become
reserved for travelling?
Head down, collar up, catch the last
bus, train, tube, if it's running.

The night is only fearsome
when approached deliberately –
like walking up to a stranger
and telling a secret
or taking a hand.

Tonight, I saw the budding of the trees
pale blossom, crisp green,
sly moonlight looking through
smoke-blue Battersea sky,
and I was laughing:

I didn't know the spring arrived at night.
I didn't know my heart had been a ruby all along.

# STRANGE ANIMALS

# Hungarian Dogs

A Hungarian dog will greet you
on the Metro
with a look and a nod.

On the street
it will not speak
unless spoken to.

Within the confines of a yard –
painted fence, neatly trimmed hedge,
border of marigolds –
it will snap its teeth
at the barrier, defending
effusive rose bushes and
the man who carries the dog
lovingly in his arms
down the swift escalators of the M3
but still expects it to retrieve
the last stag killed.

# Your Amazing All-Inclusive Holiday Getaway

tropical air, resting, livid, hums
with the weight of humidity, gossiping
crickets and the confidence of palms

*look at them*, remark the mosquitoes
with strength in numbers, teeth bared to the night,
*these are Northern people*

staring squint-eyed at the sun, pinking skin
exposed, they lack indifference to heat,
playacting roles of knowing

as they lie supine on the sand
eat beyond fullness, drink past thirst,
tracing the sun across ribs and clavicles

red turns to brown, peels back again to white, until
they must return to their Northern places, static
surging through dry fingertips and thin, silky hair

*quick now, drink them*, say the mosquitoes,
smelling frost and mangoes in their skin,
raising wings in a farewell toast: *drink to our deaths*

# Rock Doves

The rock doves are breeding on the old Elysium.
Hens playing hard to get,
hopping along the cracked balustrade,
looking over shoulders, aloof and eager,
at the cocks strutting on the chimney tops.

They peer down from their parliament
at the trainside brothel and the stumblers,
high on the High Street, oblivious to the wind,
ruffling feathers for quick coitus on the ledge.

This building is beautiful – look at her
regal windows, fine brickwork,
gold-etched marble over the chained and boarded door.
Tarted up for the bingo and used by the labour men,
now saplings grow from her cracked cornices
and green wire netting tries to keep the rock doves at bay.

But they are roosting, rutting, rooting into her
fine lines and softening stone.
They doze in her dormers
and claim her highest peaks each hour,
knowing theirs is the best view of the sea.

# Battersea, Sunday Evening

woman sitting on doorstep
smoking, looking
at the moon

one empty wine glass, next to
man in pub with newspaper
and one full (red)

two dogs at traffic lights
sit in unison until
the light changes

three boys walking
one stops, dances before me
we smile, walk on

# Woodlouse on the Bathroom Floor, Last Words

*Google search: why are there dead woodlice in my house?*

*Result:* **Woodlice** *will die in most home environments as they are damp lovers and are soon dehydrated by our warm indoor environments. (pestcontroldirect.co.uk)*

How did I get here?
And why have I come?

It looked so promising
on the cold, dark journey
through the wall.

I am so thirsty.

I'll just lie here a minute,
put my feet up, think of
my prehistoric ancestors
fossilized in stone.

# Prisms

gemstones that crown my finger
    catch autumn light
    create eighteen prisms on the wall
rainbow and white while water
in a glass laps at the rim
like tides in a clean bay at low sun
easily seen grains of sand
    or wood beneath the glass another
trick of vision that the cat tries to catch
crueller than the fireflies in summer
flicking their switches off-and-on
in the night at least we know
    they are really there
but I don't tell her now in the warm room
wild eyes darting paws pouncing her best
    reflexes spent on lying light
until a cloud passes the window
dousing the game and the pair of us
in afternoon shadow.

# Strange Animals

My kitten likes to chew
zippers, electrical cords,
corrugated cardboard,
the spider plant in the bathroom,
spines of books, wooden table legs,
socks fresh out of warm shoes,
skin that smells of soap,
her sister's ear,
my hand,
nuzzling, focused, fervent searching
for her mother's nipple,
weaned too soon,
new sharp teeth
make bruises on my palm
that I endure with the patience of
a mother's love.

# Gypsy Moth

The gypsy moths descended, crawling
over highways and dumpsters, swing sets and cars,
their munching and dropping of frass
the sound of rain
defoliating every tree in Ontario.

It was even on the news;
Adults were alarmed, *this is it*
they said,
but no one knew where *it*
had come from, a soft creeping thing
patterned like a Gypsy's skirt,
blue and yellow and green and red.
I remember the blue best
but it is not my memory because
a Google search shows hairy brown stripes
and blue is not common in nature.

At recess we adopted them from trees.
I would be a Gypsy for Halloween, not knowing
that culture is not a costume.
My grandpa said you can't trust a Gypsy;
they take blonde little children like us, like I had taken
my caterpillar. I named him Fatso; I think I knew
that was unkind. But
I petted his back, put him in my desk
with the pencil shavings, a good home.
I didn't understand that Fatso didn't understand,
*Now stay here.*

We had a lesson, French songs or colouring
when Becky's sandal slid across the floor between our desks,
yellow slime, a scream, a hoard
inching intrepid down table legs

escaping us; it escaped us
that our teachers saw
a room full of caterpillars and children,
my God, can you imagine
a room full of us that might never
cocoon or grow wings.

# Hungarian Skies

Are always telling stories:

A tempest rolling in will first be painted;
watercolour wash of deep indigo
down to steam rising from the belly
of the slain boar split open before the copper green
onion-domed church and the people of Lipót
preparing the *bogrács* and evening disco.

But with a breath of warm winds
heavy with the dust of scythes and ragweed
now the blue sky you will recognize
from Szinyei Merse Pál's *Pacsirta*
and the clouds all *Erdélyi* embroidery
picked by deft, gnarled hands.

And later, in the 18th district walking home
from the post office silhouetted against
swathes of sunset silk, my scrim
peach mid-winter dusk,
having sent parcels of marzipan
and crossword puzzles to Grandpa,
I won't be angry at the woman
who charges me more for stamps
every time.

# The Sailor and the Shepherd

*Red sky at night, sailors' delight.*

It's a shepherd, you say. Landlocked.

*Red sky at morning, sailors take warning.*

But what about the sheep?

The clouds have dreamed, gone with the flame.
So, the sun has set.
Everything is coloured like the sea.

*What now?* I ask.
You shrug, go back to walking your same old hills.

# Woman seeking Man 28-42

Not looking for a pen pal
Like the usual stuff really
Gym, keep fit, tattoos
Nights out with the boys
Love a bit o' banter
HATE filters! Sorry girls
If u don't look like ur picture ur buying the drinks til you do
I've got 2 kids they are my world
Message me to know more
If your not gonna talk don't swipe right!!!
Just a genuine nice guy
Are there any <u>honest</u> women left out there???
New to this
Not sure what to put here lol
6'2" save you asking
5'7" 'cause apparently that's important
No time wasters
Love dogs
Looking for my partner in crime
Looking for a travel buddy → doing up a campervan
Love a cheeky takeaway
Just got out of a long-term relationship
Seeing how this goes
Kid is my nephew
Enjoy spending time with family and friends
Like music and films
Recently divorced
job ☑
car ☑
house ☑
Looking for someone who doesn't take themselves too seriously
My friends describe me as
easy-going, intelligent, witty
LOYAL and HUMBLE

Married but looking for a little bit extra
Only human
Enjoy socialising
If we don't match, don't be offended
If u think u can't handle me swipe left
No drama
Hoping to meet new people
Good girls need not apply

# Found in Swansea

Mangled umbrella, bin (x3, Singleton Park, one day in November)

Blood on pavement (Oxford Street, Saturday 6pm)

Whole chicken, raw (Brynmill Park, afternoon)

Love (x2, Eaton Crescent)

Excrement, not canine (bus stop, Gors Avenue)

Women's underpants, wet from rain (stone wall, Nyanza Terrace)

Slug on my pillow (Cockett, 2nd storey bedroom, 4am)

Heartbreak (x2, Eaton Crescent)

Battenburg cake (bus stop, Gors Avenue)

# Gors Avenue

The stock bus passengers
keep heads down, eyes fixed
on phones or outwards
to the windows of houses
where poverty makes the curtains sag.
Barbed wire crowns close-clustered shops:
Trenches with a takeaway.

My favourite drunk alights, singing Sinatra
at grannies who pretend not to enjoy it.
I scan crisp-packet-tinselled far off fields
for the Gypsies' ponies in the valley below.

# Toronto Retrograde

these days
nights are spent running for last streetcars
December on the cheek like a bittersweet kiss
in another country

false stars flicker in shop windows across Hogtown
as I search the sky for Venus
tap

      dance

            down

                  aged

                        stairwells

leaving figure-8s in the salted frost

between shifts the basement dwellers
never know the sun
daylight costs extra when you're counting tips
thirty-three cents on a bowl of soup and a bad attitude

awaiting the solstice on the 510 Spadina
Orion's Belt stretches over the crow sky
reminding me they were the only stars
I could count on
those nights in Brynmill

# so green and quick and urgent

what do I lament?

lives lived on rooftops

a fear of heights
that is really
a fear of falling

too much time spent in cities, alone

still, I hold trees for strength
chart myself by the moon
read rivers and listen for clues
in birdsong and rain and the wind

it speaks as I listen
opens magnolias and moves
the salt river, so green and quick and urgent
even the birds must skip
to stay ahead

# Hungarian Applause

is a beating heart.

Slow, steady, rising rhythm…
like watching the approach
of a past lover
from across a crowded room.

Faster! It races
The Singular Audience
a collective consciousness, a village drum
and Boom! Uproar meets Crescendo –

We all understand how this works.

On stage, two American banjo players
watch, wait, ask
like curious children,
'What does that mean?'

The collective laughs. Claps again.
We get our encore.

# Dog Year

This is the end of my dog year.
Seven winters of trying
to till frozen soil. Didn't you know?
Summers can be cold even in a drought.
I kept watching the cracks in my heartland
travelling, reaching out to each jagged *inukshuk*:
But how do you make fire with only shards of flint?

I am tired of being
on the closed side of the gate.
How did I get here?
Safe in my salt circle, sure,
but who can come in?
And how to get out?

Nothing has gone according to plan.

Let's start with spring:
Lighter mornings mean easier nights.
Hyacinth perfumes the bedside, daffodils
even prettier curled to crêpe paper.
Read. Stretch.
Open the window when the day is fine.

Next step.

Knee-deep in the tundra of Aurora
the darkness is blue, not black.
Standing at the precipice of Salzburg's salted alps
the clouds rest only for me.
Climbing to the peak at Visegrád
is my entire life, up and out.

And now this,
whipped and whetted by the winds of Rhossili
for better or worse, this
is where the light breaks through.

# RIVER READING

# I.

## Queens, Minor Arcana

This is you right now.

A queen of the senses;
shades of sweet green, yarrow,
stars in a sunlit sky.

When all of a sudden
the trees have leafed –
a clean white feather at your feet
and you cannot see
the sea.

## II.
## Five of Cups

But three spilt,
your obstacle:

those old griefs
bereft, too long –
yes, you married each, but
they didn't marry you back.

When did you last read the river?

Now take off your mourning cloak
and drink.

# III.
## Ten of Pentacles

This is your foundation:
thank father and mother for
the jingling coins and old homestead,
the well-fed cats;
brother and his babies.

Creeks still run high in the spring.

You can keep on leaving;
they will never leave you.

# IV.
## Ten of Cups

This is your ideal:
love and children dancing.

All the cups are filled.

See the house in the distance?
It's at the end of a river.

If you follow the current, does it lead to
a lake or a sea?

# V.
## Three of Wands

Your beloved bay recedes.
It's time to go, the ships are coming in.

But oh, still you cling
to the echo of his tenor,
all *hiraeth*, all ache.

Your three loves,
that grew as if by magic, now
washed away with the winter run-off
and the rubbish that rides
the tides.

# VI.
## Six of Swords

In your near future you are travelling.
Dying, too.

This is the space between
the end and the beginning.

From Tawe to Danube, and ever Niagara,
no longer reading the river
but riding it:

the path is made of water
but the boat is heavy with steel.

# VII.
## The Fool

This is how you see yourself:

wise enough to leap
from the cliff, but
fool enough to guess
where you're going.

Pack your satchel
and bring along your familiars.

Do not be afraid to look
straight at the sun.

# VIII.
## Seven of Wands

This is how others see you:

balancing on that hill
always alone, outnumbered
but winning, they suppose, because
what else is there to do?

This is your environment,
on stage again.

Head first to the wind, sure,
but only when the rains come.

# IX.
## The Tower

This is what you fear
and what you hope for:

to jump
from the burning tower
or, to roll
over the falls in a barrel.

Either way, something changes.

Every bone is broken,
but washed clean, too.

# X.
# The Empress

Outcome: not a queen,
but an Empress.

Perpetually pregnant,
oh yes, it is time
for birth and for heat.

Look closer –
there, in the distance,
your Niagara moving rushing
emotion erosion.

You have found your river run,
see how your garden grows.

# River Reading

**IV.**

This is your ideal:
love and children dancing.
All the cups are filled.
See the house in the
distance?
It's at the end of a river.
If you follow the current,
does it lead to
a lake or a sea?

**I.i**

**This is you right now.
A queen of the senses;
shades of sweet green,
yarrow,
stars in a sunlit sky.**

**V.**

Your beloved bay recedes.
It's time to go,
the ships are coming in.

But oh, still you cling
to the echo of his tenor,
all *hiraeth*, all ache.

Your three loves,
that grew as if by magic,
now washed away
with the winter run off
and the rubbish that rides
the tides.

**II.**

But three spilt,
your obstacle:

those old griefs
bereft, too long –
yes, you married each, but
they didn't marry you
back.

When did you last read the
river?

Now take off your
mourning cloak
and drink.

**I.ii**

**When all of a sudden
the trees have leafed –
a clean white feather
at your feet
and you cannot see
the sea.**

**III.**

This is your foundation:
thank father and mother
for the jingling coins and
old homestead,
the well-fed cats,
brother and his babies.
Creeks still run high in the
spring.

You can keep on leaving;
they will never leave you.

**VI.**

In your near future
you are travelling.
Dying, too.

This is the space between
the end and the beginning.
From Tawe to Danube,
and ever Niagara,
no longer reading the river
but riding it:

the path is made of water
but the boat is heavy with
steel.

**X.**

Outcome: not a queen,
but an Empress.
Perpetually pregnant,
oh yes, it is time
for birth and for heat.

Look closer –
there, in the distance,
your Niagara moving
rushing emotion erosion.
You have found your
river run,
see how your garden
grows.

**IX.**

This is what you fear
and what you hope for:
to jump
from the burning
tower.
or to roll
over the falls in a barrel.

Either way,
something changes.
Every bone is broken,
but washed clean, too.

**VIII.**

This is how others see you:
balancing on that hill,
always alone, outnumbered
but winning, they suppose,
because
what else is there to do?

This is your environment,
on stage again.
Head first to the wind,
sure, but only when
the rains come.

**VII.**

This is how you see
yourself:
wise enough to leap
from the cliff, but
fool enough to guess
where you're going.
Pack your satchel
and bring along
your familiars.
Do not be afraid to look
straight at the sun.

# Notes on Poems

### Itthon
*itthon*: at home
*cukrászda*: confectionary café
*dobos torta, Eszterházy, geszténye puré*: chocolate drum cake, walnut cake, chestnut purée

### Things I Have Learned About Planting a Garden
*zöldbableves*: Hungarian green bean soup

### On Christmas Eve
*pogácsa*: yeasted sour cream scones
*smörgåsbord*: Swedish feast table
*Gewürztraminer*: sweet German wine
*kachelofen*: ceramic wood stove

### Meeting Emily Carr in the Bush
Emily Carr (1871-1945) was a Canadian artist who painted scenes depicting indigenous themes and landscapes of the Pacific Northwest.

### My uncles are dying
*nem végállomás*: 'not the last stop'
*Következő megálló*: 'next stop'

### tan-renga and a haiku, for Nigel Jenkins
The first two haiku are by the late Nigel Jenkins, appearing in his collection *Blue* (Planet, 2002). I have used them to create tan-renga, by adding two lines to each poem.

### Loose Jewels
*zsírós kenyér*: bread with lard, raw onion, and paprika.
Nefelejcs utca: Forget-me-not Road, Pestszentlőrinc, 18th District Budapest
*Kezit csókolom kívánok*: formal greeting, 'I wish to kiss your hand'
*temető*: cemetery
*Édesanya*: respectful endearment, 'sweet mother'

**In the Land of Fairies**
Ironstone is a sedimentary rock containing a high proportion of iron.
'fossilized star' refers to star-shaped crinoid fossils, which can be found in
some UK rivers and were once believed to be 'fairy coins'.

**Rock Doves**
The 'Elysium' is a building on Swansea High Street. It opened in 1914 as
Elysium Cinema, and has also been used as a dock workers' hall and bingo
hall. It has been vacant (of human use) since 1994.

**Hungarian Skies**
*bogrács*: cauldron for cooking stew
*Pacsirta*: *Nightingale* by Szinyei Merse Pál (oil on canvas, c.1882, Hungarian
National Gallery)
*Erdélyi*: Transylvanian

**Dog Year**
*Inukshuk*: Inuit stone man

**Five of Cups**
*hiraeth*: homesickness, deep longing, grief.

**River Reading**
The sequence is modelled after the Celtic Cross tarot reading spread, with
each poem symbolising one of ten cards. The positions of the cards have the
following designations: 1. The subject of the reading/person for whom it is
being read; 2. Obstacle or Influence; 3. Foundation/Subconscious; 4.
Ideal/Conscious mind; 5. What is receding; 6. The near future; 7. Your role or
attitude; 8. Your environment or how others see you; 9. Hopes and Fears; 10.
The Outcome of the query.

# Acknowledgements

Earlier versions of some of these poems have been published elsewhere:

'Orienteering' appeared in *New Welsh Review*, and in the poetry pamphlet *Loose Jewels* (Cinnamon Press, 2020).

'Loose Jewels' appeared in *Arc Poetry Magazine*, and in *Loose Jewels* (Cinnamon Press, 2020).

The following poems also appeared in *Loose Jewels* (Cinnamon Press, 2020): 'Itthon', 'On Christmas Eve', 'In Praise of Great Lake Swimmers', 'Bears Only Want to Love Their Children', 'National Parks and Reserves', 'My uncles are dying' (as 'Uncles'), 'What season do the buzzards come?', 'Leftovers', 'Hungarian Dogs', 'Hungarian Skies', 'Hungarian Applause', and 'Dog Year'.

'Rock Doves' appeared in *The Lampeter Review*.

'Queens (Minor Arcana)', 'Three of Wands', 'The Fool', and 'The Tower' from the 'River Reading' sequence appear in *In the Voice of Trees: an anthology of tree lore* (Cinnamon Press, 2020).

Huge thanks to my friends and first readers for their advice, encouragement, and willingness to dig into a poem with me: Rhys Owain Williams, Richard Jones, Mari Ellis Dunning, Rae Howells, The Salty Poets and the Hay Writers at Work, and my sharp-eyed editor Susie Wildsmith. Thanks also to everyone at Parthian and to Lieke van der Vorst for allowing us to use her wonderful illustration for the cover. And all my love and gratitude to my family, for teaching me how to tell stories and allowing me to share theirs, and especially to my mum, for understanding, and to my dad, for everything.

# PARTHIAN *Poetry*

## Windfalls
### Susie Wild
ISBN 978-1-912681-75-4
£9 | Paperback

'Powerful, beautifully crafted poems...
there's nothing like poetry to cut down the spaces
between us, to leap across gaps,
make a friend of a stranger.'
— **Jonathan Edwards**

## Small
### Natalie Ann Holborow
ISBN 978-1-912681-76-1
£9 | Paperback

'Shoot for the moon? Holborow has landed, roamed its face,
dipped into the craters, and gathered an armful of stars
while up there.'
— **Wales Arts Review**

## The Language of Bees
### Rae Howells
ISBN 978-1-913640-69-9
£9 | Paperback
'rich in love, for the world that we are inseparable from
and on the verge of destroying.'
— **Matthew Francis**